JAPANESE MYTHOLOGY

Susanoo

BY HEATHER C. HUDAK

CONTENT CONSULTANT
CALEB CARTER, PhD
ASSOCIATE PROFESSOR OF JAPANESE RELIGIONS
AND BUDDHIST STUDIES
KYUSHU UNIVERSITY

Kids Core
An Imprint of Abdo Publishing
abdobooks.com

abdobooks.com

Printed in the United States of America, North Mankato, Minnesota.
102024
012025

THIS BOOK CONTAINS RECYCLED MATERIALS

Cover Photo: Shutterstock Images
Interior Photos: Art Collection 2/Alamy, 4–5, 29 (top); Yukari Mishima/Shutterstock Images, 7; Pictures from History/Universal Images Group/Getty Images, 8; Carla Silene/Shutterstock Images, 10; Shutterstock Images, 12–13, 15 (top left), 15 (top right), 15 (bottom left), 15 (bottom middle), 15 (bottom right), 16, 22, 24, 25, 28 (top), 29 (bottom); Stephen Coyne/Alamy, 18; MeijiShowa/Alamy, 20–21, 28 (bottom); Heritage Art/Heritage Images/Hulton Archive/Getty Images, 26

Editor: Christa Kelly
Series Designer: Ryan Gale

Library of Congress Control Number: 2024938347

Publisher's Cataloging-in-Publication Data

Names: Hudak, Heather C., author.
Title: Susanoo / by Heather C. Hudak
Description: Minneapolis, Minnesota: ABDO Publishing, 2025 | Series: Japanese mythology | Includes online resources and index.
Identifiers: ISBN 9781098295981 (lib. bdg.) | ISBN 9798384916987 (ebook)
Subjects: LCSH: Mythology, Japanese--Juvenile literature. | Deities--Juvenile literature. | Susanoo (Shinto deity)--Juvenile literature. | Susanoo no Mikoto (Shinto deity)--Juvenile literature. | Mythology, Asian—Juvenile literature.
Classification: DDC 398.21--dc23

CONTENTS

CHAPTER 1
The Eight-Headed Dragon 4

CHAPTER 2
Susanoo the Troublemaker 12

CHAPTER 3
Power and Importance 20

Legendary Facts 28
Glossary 30
Online Resources 31
Learn More 31
Index 32
About the Author 32

Kushinadahime, *bottom*, was the daughter of Ashinazuchi and Tenazuchi, *middle*. She met the god Susanoo, *top*.

CHAPTER 1

The Eight-Headed Dragon

Susanoo (pronounced soo-sah-no-oh) was a god. He ruled the ocean and storms. One day, he went for a walk along a river. There, he met a mother, a father, and their child. They were crying. Susanoo asked why they were sad.

The family told him they once had eight daughters. Each year, a giant, eight-headed dragon called Yamata no Orochi ate one of the girls. The family had only one daughter left. Her name was Kushinadahime (koo-shee-nah-duh-hee-may). They feared the dragon would come for her soon.

Susanoo offered to help the family. In exchange, he asked to marry their daughter. The family accepted. Susanoo turned the girl into a comb. He put the comb in his hair for safekeeping. He then told the mother and father to build a fence around their house. He said the fence should have eight gates, one for each of the dragon's heads. He told the family to place a sweet drink inside each gate to lure the dragon.

Each of Yamata no Orochi's heads had blood-red eyes.

The parents quickly followed Susanoo's advice. Then, they waited. After a little while, the dragon appeared. Each of its heads went into a separate gate to drink the sweet bait.

Susanoo lured Yamata no Orochi with a rice drink called sake (SAH-kee).

The dragon was tired after drinking. It fell asleep. Susanoo chose that moment to attack. He cut off all eight of the dragon's heads and tails. One of the tails was very hard to cut through. Susanoo finally sliced it off. Inside was a sword covered in jewels. Susanoo gave the sword to his sister. Then, he married Kushinadahime.

Ancient Stories

Japan is a country in eastern Asia. Japanese people have been telling stories about gods and monsters for hundreds of years.

Written Records

At first, Japanese mythology was told aloud. People heard the stories and told their families and friends. The stories were first written down in about 700 CE. The oldest written records about Japan are called *Kojiki* and *Nihon Shoki*. These books talk about the **imperial** family. They also include **traditional** Shinto myths.

Sculptures in Japan depict Susanoo's battle with Yamata no Orochi.

Some of these stories describe the creation of Japan. Others explain why natural events happen. These **traditional** stories are called myths.

Myths are an important part of Shinto. Shinto is a Japanese religion. The religion centers around *kami*, or "spirits." Gods are kami. So are some monsters. Animals and plants can be kami, too.

Susanoo is one of the most famous kami. More than a thousand years after his stories were first told, he remains an important part of Japanese mythology.

Explore Online

Visit the website below. Does it give any new information about Shinto that wasn't in Chapter One?

Shinto

abdocorelibrary.com/susanoo

Izanami, *left*, and Izanagi, *right*, created the islands of Japan.

CHAPTER 2

Susanoo the Troublemaker

Susanoo is the son of the gods Izanagi and Izanami. One day, Izanagi went to a river to clean himself. As he did, he created three gods. Amaterasu (ah-mah-teh-rah-soo) was born when Izanagi washed his left eye.

Tsukuyomi (soo-kee-yo-mee) was born when Izanagi washed his right eye. Susanoo was born when he washed his nose.

Izanagi made Amaterasu the goddess of the sun. He made Tsukuyomi the god of the moon. He made Susanoo the god of the seas and storms.

Causing Trouble

Amaterasu and Tsukuyomi were obedient. But Susanoo was unpredictable. He did not obey Izanagi. He wanted his mother, but she was in the underworld. He cried so much that the mountains shrank and the seas dried up. Izanagi became angry. He **banished** Susanoo to rule the land of the dead.

Susanoo Family Tree

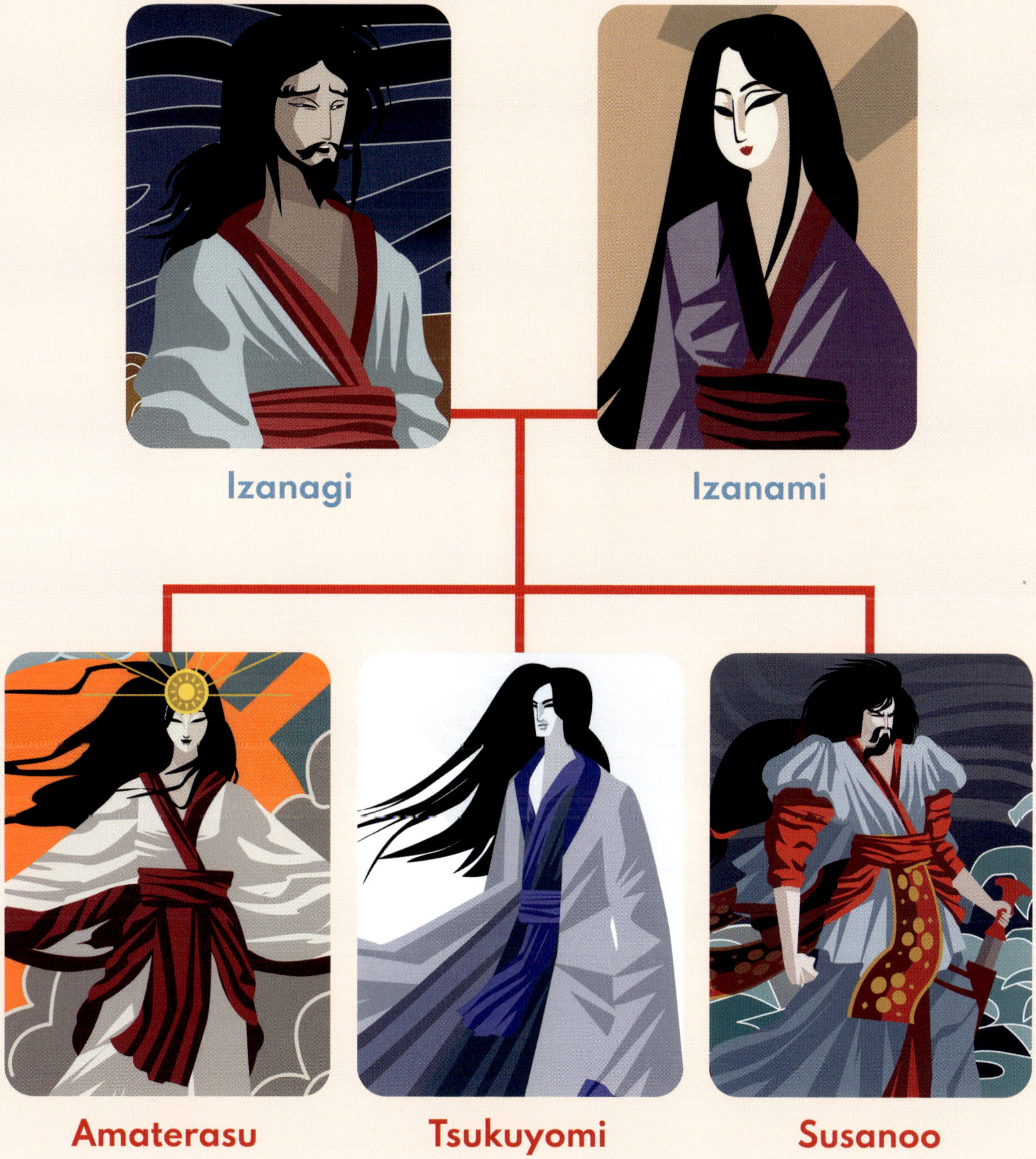

Susanoo was often considered the outcast of his family.

Before Susanoo was banished, stories described him as cruel and wicked.

Before Susanoo left, he went to say goodbye to Amaterasu. They got into a fight. Susanoo destroyed Amaterasu's rice fields. He wrecked her weaving. Amaterasu was so upset that she shut herself in a cave and refused to come out. The world went dark. The other kami eventually lured her back out. They then cast Susanoo out of heaven for his bad behavior.

Becoming a Hero

Susanoo later began to change his ways. He killed the eight-headed dragon to save Kushinadahime. He became kinder and gentler. He gave Amaterasu the jeweled sword that he had found in the dragon's tail as a peace offering. The sword became one of the three **sacred** treasures of Japan.

Japanese Imperial Regalia

Amaterasu gave Susanoo's sword to her grandson Ninigi. She also gave him a jewel and a mirror. These three treasures are called the imperial **regalia**. Amaterasu then sent Ninigi to rule on Earth. To this day, every new **emperor** of Japan is presented with the imperial regalia.

Okuninushi is a celebrated figure in Japan.

After killing the dragon, Susanoo and Kushinadahime built a palace in a place called Suga. Susanoo and Kushinadahime had many children who grew up to be powerful kami. Their son Okuninushi was especially powerful. He was the leader of the earthly kami. Later, he became the god of the underworld.

Primary Source

Susanoo missed his mother so much that horrible things started to happen to the world. His father, Izanagi, told Susanoo:

> You can no longer live in this country. If you were to rule this land, the lives of many people would be taken from them. It would be best if you were to rule the Land of [the Dead].

Source: Gary P. Leupp and De-min Tao, editors. *The Tokugawa World*. Routledge, 2021, p. 845.

What's the Big Idea?

Read the primary source text carefully. What is its main idea? Explain how the main idea is supported by details.

Today, people still tell stories about Susanoo's adventures.

CHAPTER 3

Power and Importance

Susanoo is very important to Japanese people. Some people consider him the god of farming. He is often linked to rice fields. People used to pray to him for a good harvest. They also prayed to him to bring rain and keep away disease and illness.

People visit Yaegaki Shrine to pray for romance, health, and safety.

Sailors would pray to Susanoo to keep the seas calm.

The love between Susanoo and Kushinadahime still inspires people today. People pray to the couple for relationship advice. Others ask Susanoo and Kushinadahime to bless their marriage or help them find a partner.

Sacred Places

Japan has many shrines to honor Susanoo. A shrine is a sacred space dedicated to a god or holy person. When people go to a shrine, they are visiting the person the shrine honors. Yaegaki Shrine is in Matsue, Japan. It is dedicated to Susanoo and his wife. According to legend, Yaegaki is where Susanoo and Kushinadahime were married.

Mirror Pond

There is a small pool called Mirror Pond at Yaegaki Shrine. Some people believe Kushinadahime's spirit lives in the pond. People place a piece of paper in the water and then put a coin on the paper. If it sinks quickly, they will find love soon.

According to legend, Suga Shrine is where *waka*, a form of Japanese poetry, was invented.

Suga Shrine is also dedicated to Susanoo and his wife. The shrine is in Tokyo, Japan. It marks where the couple built their palace.

Susa Shrine is in Izumo, Japan. It honors the place where Susanoo laid his soul to rest and became one with nature. People believe that his soul roams the valley around the shrine.

Yasaka Shrine is in Kyoto, Japan. It is dedicated to Susanoo, Kushinadahime, and their children. Cords hang from large bells in the shrine's main hall. Pulling the cords lets

Yasaka Shrine was founded more than 1,300 years ago.

the gods know people are there to worship. People come to Yasaka to pray for protection from evil and disasters. They also pray for good health and ask Susanoo to keep them safe from diseases.

Many Japanese artworks are made by carving images into wood. The carved wood is then covered in ink to make a stamp.

Susanoo in Art

People have honored Susanoo with art for hundreds of years. Many Japanese artworks show Susanoo killing the eight-headed dragon. Several Japanese plays also feature the storm god.

Susanoo appears in pop culture too. There are many characters based on Susanoo in Japanese cartoons and comic books. Some video games include the god.

Susanoo remains an important Shinto god. More than a thousand years after his birth, myths about Susanoo are still passed down from one generation to the next. People continue to honor Susanoo throughout Japan and the world.

Further Evidence

Look at the website below. Does it give any new evidence to support Chapter Three?

Yaegaki Shrine

abdocorelibrary.com/susanoo

Legendary Facts

Susanoo is the Japanese god of storms and the sea.

Susanoo often got in fights with his family. After upsetting his sister Amaterasu, he was banished from heaven.

Susanoo married Kushinadahime, a girl he saved from an eight-headed dragon.

Today, Susanoo is honored at shrines and in artwork.

Glossary

banished
forced to leave an area

emperor
the ruler of an empire

imperial
relating to an emperor or empire

regalia
fancy clothes or accessories, often worn by royalty

sacred
describing something important, often with religious value

traditional
relating to practices from the past

Online Resources

To learn more about Susanoo and Japanese mythology, visit our free resource websites below.

Core Library CONNECTION
FREE! COMMON CORE MULTIMEDIA RESOURCES

Visit **abdocorelibrary.com** or scan this QR code for free Common Core resources for teachers and students, including vetted activities, multimedia, and booklinks, for deeper subject comprehension.

Booklinks NONFICTION NETWORK
FREE! ONLINE NONFICTION RESOURCES

Visit **abdobooklinks.com** or scan this QR code for free additional online weblinks for further learning. These links are routinely monitored and updated to provide the most current information available.

Learn More

Cornell, Kari. *Dragons of Japanese Mythology.* Abdo, 2025.

Fox, Jay. *My First Book of Japanese.* Bushel & Peck, 2022.

Golkar, Golriz. *Amaterasu.* Abdo, 2025.

Index

Amaterasu, 9, 13–14, 15, 16–17

Izanagi, 13–14, 15, 19
Izanami, 13–14, 15, 19
Izumo, 24

Kushinadahime, 5–6, 9, 17–18, 22, 23–24
Kyoto, 24

Matsue, 23

Okuninushi, 18, 24

Shinto, 9, 11, 27
shrines, 23–25, 27
Suga, 18, 24
Suga Shrine, 24
Susa Shrine, 24

Tokyo, 24
Tsukuyomi, 14, 15

Yaegaki Shrine, 23, 27
Yamata no Orochi, 6–8, 17–18, 26
Yasaka Shrine, 24–25

About the Author

Heather C. Hudak has written hundreds of books for children. She writes about all kinds of topics, from animals to ancient legends. When Heather is not writing, she loves to travel. She has been to about 60 countries, including Japan. In Japan, she visited many shrines that honor the kami of Japanese mythology.